# PRACTICAL ARNIS STICK FIGHTING

VORTEX CONTROL STICK FIGHTING FOR SELF-DEFENSE

SAM FURY

*Illustrated by*
ELIANA BASTIDA

# WARNINGS AND DISCLAIMERS

The information in this publication is made public for reference only.

Neither the author, publisher, nor anyone else involved in the production of this publication is responsible for how the reader uses the information or the result of his/her actions.

# CONTENTS

# THANKS FOR YOUR PURCHASE

**Did you know you can get FREE chapters of any SF Nonfiction Book you want?**

https://offers.SFNonfictionBooks.com/Free-Chapters

You will also be among the first to know of FREE review copies, discount offers, bonus content, and more.

Go to:

https://offers.SFNonfictionBooks.com/Free-Chapters

Thanks again for your support.

# INTRODUCTION

In this self-defense training manual, Sam Fury puts Vortex Control Self-Defense lessons learned in the Philippines onto paper.

Vortex Control Self-Defense is a unique fighting system created by Peter Sunbye. To create this system of self-defense, Peter traveled for 20+ years, searching for "lost" self-defense techniques.

He combined a number of martial arts, including GM Lawrence Lee's Tong Kune Do kung fu, Wing Chun, Balintawak Arnis Escrima, and Panatukan to create a highly effective and relatively easy to learn self-defense system. Once the basics are learned, Vortex Control Self-Defense can be applied effectively by almost anyone, regardless of their dexterity, strength, or fitness level.

This volume covers stick fighting. Kali Arnis is a Filipino martial art based on stick-fighting. This book combines methods learnt from a variety of Kali Arnis grandmasters and focuses on highly practical stick-fighting techniques and training drills.

The Vortex Control Stick-Fighting method is primarily based on an advanced form of long- and close-range balintawak escrima arnis stick style, founded by the Rosada Lineage and directly linked back to Venancio "Anciong" Bacon. Although this system is advanced and modernized, the execution of techniques is simple in comparison to many other methods.

The information in this book is more than you'll need to become a superior stick-fighter; however, if you wish to develop further, you can. With what you'll learn here, you will be able to create an endless number of drills and training scenarios so you can hone your skills.

Vortex Control Stick-Fighting is purposefully designed to be highly effective yet easy to learn. The skills learned in this book can be applied to a wide range of stick-like items (half a pool cue, umbrella, wooden stake, stick on the ground, etc.) which makes it highly practical for self-defense and/or street fighting.

This publication has been written under the approval of Peter Sunbye.

# EXPLANATION OF TERMS

A few terms are used throughout this book to help describe the flow of movement.

## Lead/Rear Side

Your lead side is whichever side of your body is forward-most and your rear side is whichever side of your body is rear-most. For example, if you're in a right-foot-forward stance, then your right side is your lead side, and your left side is your rear side.

## Inside/Outside of Your Opponent's Guard

When your opponent's guard is up, you can place your arm either inside or outside of it.

Being inside your opponent's guard means that your limb is in between his limbs, closer to his center. Your arm is sandwiched by his.

Being outside your opponent's guard means your opponent's limbs are both to either the left or right of your limb.

The pictures demonstrate being inside/outside of your opponent's guard with your arms, but it also applies to your legs. That is, you need to step to the outside of your opponent's guard in order to get behind him.

Just as you can be inside or outside your opponent's guard, he can be inside/outside yours.

## Guarding Your Opponent's Limb

The expression "to guard your opponent's limb" means to put your limb close or on his limb so that you can't be struck by it. It is a pre-emptive defensive maneuver that may also be referred to as "covering your opponent's limb."

Throughout this book, the word "limb" is replaced as appropriate. For example, in the previous picture the man is using his right hand to guard/cover the woman's right elbow.

## Changing Grip

Changing grip (a.k.a. switching grip) means shifting from an over-hand grip on your opponent's stick to an underhand one. Doing this will make it easier to perform certain actions. Whichever way your palm faces is the direction that will be easiest for you to push, hence making it easier to snatch.

**Note:** Snatching is when you disarm your opponent. It is explained in detail later on in this book.

This means, assuming your opponent is in a structurally correct position, you can anticipate what he will do by noting the direction his palm faces.

The best way to change grip is to first push the stick into your opponent's face. This will cause him pain and will also bring you to his center, which will make it harder for him to move back.

When grabbing low, it is preferable to use an underhand grip. You can snatch more easily, and the grip exposes your muscle rather than your bone, so if your opponent hits your arm it will not hurt as much.

**Jumping Hands**

Jumping hands is moving your hand from a high position on your opponent's stick to a low position, or vice versa. It is necessary to do this in order to create opportunities for yourself or to prevent your opponent from snatching your stick.

If you just try to jump from high to low, or vice versa, your opponent can pull his stick back, so that you miss. To prevent this, push your opponent's, stick towards him a little before jumping. The natural reaction of your opponent will be to push back because he will not want to get hit in the face. Make the jump when your opponent does this push back.

# PRINCIPLES OF SELF-DEFENSE

The following principles are the core of Vortex Control Self-Defense. Although explained in reference to hand-to-hand combat, they are also applicable to weaponry.

Without these principles, the rest of this book is just a bunch of techniques that you can mimic. With them, the techniques in this book become a collection of examples of how the principles can be applied. You can then replicate techniques and/or create customized to ones.

The Vortex Control Self-Defense principles are all of equal importance, and are presented here in alphabetical order.

## Constant Barrage

In Vortex Control Self-Defense there, you are constantly slapping, twisting, pulling, and pushing your opponent. This serves at least one (and usually several, if not all) of the following purposes:

- It confuses and disorients your opponent.
- It often lets you move your opponent one way while striking from the opposite direction. This increases the force of your strike.
- The movements in themselves bring a certain degree of discomfort and pain.
- It lets you place your opponent in the ideal position for your next move.

This also makes use of Newton's first law of motion, which states that:

> "An object at rest stays at rest, and an object in motion stays in motion with the same speed and in the same direction unless acted upon by an unbalanced force."

In reference to your movement, this means that it's better for you to keep moving once you're in motion. This is because it takes more energy to stop and restart than it does to continue an existing motion. In addition, the continued motion will be faster and therefore more powerful than if you were to start from inertia.

## Counters

In martial arts, a counter is an attack made in response to your opponent's attack. It is about being proactive.

There is always a counter to your opponent's move, and there is a counter to your counter, and a counter to that counter. It can go on forever. The victor will be whoever has the foresight and/or intuition to out-counter their opponent.

Close combat is a game of chess. Fast chess. Instinctive chess.

**Note:** The closer you get to your opponent, the fewer opportunities there are for counters. You can use this to your advantage by first closing distance while gaining an advantageous position, and then finishing the fight before your opponent recovers.

## Grounding

Grounding yourself means being in solid contact with the ground.

When you're grounded, you have more stability, and can therefore generate more powerful attacks. Power in strikes comes up from the ground. This is a well-known concept in the world of martial arts.

A simple exercise you can do to get the feeling of grounding is to pretend that you're drilling your body into the ground.

The act of grounding can also be used to increase damage by letting gravity do the work. To get the feeling of using grounding in this manner, lift both your legs off the ground without jumping. Just let gravity do its thing.

## Fulcrums

Body mechanics, paired with physics, play a big part in the efficiency of Vortex Control Self-Defense. By using parts of your body as fulcrums, you can gain more leverage, apply locks, break limbs, etc.

## One-Handed Fighting

Both arms are used in the demonstrations in this book, but the unarmed portion of Vortex Control Self-Defense is developed so that most of the techniques can be done one-handed. This becomes extremely useful in real-life scenarios, such as when you are holding something you can't drop, like a baby, or when your arm gets injured. Once you have a good grasp of the techniques, you should train to do them with one hand. Just don't use your rear hand.

## Power Angles

This is another principle based on physics and body mechanics.

There are certain angles that create the strongest frames. Your limbs should never be below 120° or above 160°.

120° is best for defense. Any smaller of an angle, and your arm will easily collapse when it's pushed towards you.

160° is best for attack. Any larger of an angle, and your arm can be easily pushed to the side. Holding it at an angle greater than 160° will also make it more susceptible to being captured—by being placed in a lock, for example.

As a rule, keep your limb at 120°. When you strike, extend it to 160° and then let your body push through. This combines power angles with grounding. Add in spring-loading and aim for the spine and you have the ideal the Vortex Control Self-Defense strike.

**Spine Center**

The Spine Center principle is based on the centerline theory, which is common in many martial arts, including Wing Chun. To explain the concept, here is an excerpt from the book *Basic Wing Chun Training* by Sam Fury:

www.SFNonfictionBooks.com/Basic-Wing-Chun-Training

Your centerline is an imaginary line drawn vertically down the center of your body. All the vital organs are located near the center of the body. Keep it away from your opponent by angling it away from him/her.

Controlling the position of your centerline in relation to your opponent's is done with footwork. Understanding the centerline will allow you to instinctively know where your opponent is.

Your central line (different from your centerline) is drawn from your angled center to your opponent.

Offensively, you generate the most power when punching out from your center, since you can incorporate your whole body and hips.

When you're attacking in a straight line, your centerline should face away from your opponent, while your central line faces his/her center.

With hook punches and other circular attacks, the center- and central lines merge.

There are three main guidelines for the centerline.

- The one who controls the centerline will control the fight.
- Protect and maintain your own centerline while you control and exploit your opponent's.
- Control the centerline by occupying it.

~

In Vortex Control Self-Defense, instead of putting your offensive focus on your opponent's centerline as described above, focus on his spine. Doing so makes the idea of striking through your target more intuitive. An added advantage is that his spine can be affected by the many jerks, twists, etc. that are commonly used in Vortex Control Self-Defense.

## Spring-Loading

Yet another principle based on the combination of body mechanics and physics is spring-loading.

The basic premise is that your muscles can be pushed in like a spring. These springs are then released in strikes, increasing speed and therefore power.

Speed in strikes is not just about how fast you reach the target. You must also be quick to recover. Recovery is the process of reloading the spring, which you can then send out again. In your arm, your triceps are the spring forward and your biceps are the spring back. Alternating spring-loading your arms allows you to make multiple strikes in very quick succession.

You can and should also spring-load your legs.

It's important to remain relaxed. The spring is loaded and released, but never tensed so much that it slows you down.

## Taking Space

Always crowd your opponent. Get in his space and claim it. Constantly push him back, and don't let up. This will unbalance him both mentally and physically.

## Following the Thank You Principle

Take whatever your opponent gives you and use it to your advantage. If he applies pressure in a particular direction, flow with it. Redirect it if needed, but don't directly oppose it.

Those that want to become really good at this are encouraged to practice Chi Sao. Although live instruction is always preferred, the book *How to do Chi Sao* by Sam Fury is highly recommended.

www.SFNonfictionBooks.com/Chi-Sao

Another use of the thank you principle is to always take something back. For example, when retracting your limb from a strike, grab your opponent's arm or nose-ring.

## Vibrating

In Vortex Control Self-Defense, the principle of vibrating is used to enhance the effectiveness of movement. It can be applied in many situations, such as when you're increasing the force in locks, making repetitive strikes, escaping holds, etc.

The following examples offer safe demonstrations of the effectiveness of vibrating:

The first example is a shirt-grab escape. Say an attacker grabs you by the shirt-front. Reach over his arms and grab his right wrist. At the same time, use your left hand to grab the same arm.

To release your opponent's grip, twist your body to your right using a waterfall motion.

This move itself is a common and effective self-defense technique, but when your attacker is much stronger than you, it may not work. Increase its effectiveness by vibrating.

As you twist your body, make small, fast, jerking movements. Concentrate these movements into your twisting motion, especially where your opponent is gripping you.

The next example is a rear bear hug escape. Say an attacker puts you in a rear bear hug with your arms pinned. A common way to get out of this is with rear elbows, but if your opponent's grip is too tight, you won't have the room to do this. Vibrate your body to create space.

As soon as you have even just enough room, rear elbow left and then right. Finally, drop your body weight and ground yourself to break your opponent's grip.

**Vortex**

By using the motion of a vortex (like water going down a sinkhole) you can easily break through your opponent's defense. For example, if your opponent is pushing your hand in a certain direction, you can use a vortex motion to move under and around it. This is actually the basis of the curve entry.

Another way to use the vortex is if your opponent grabs your arm. A fast vortex motion will most likely free you from his grip while you counter-strike in the same motion. In most cases, you'll want to vortex towards your opponent's spine.

**Warfare Strategy**

The strategy for attack in Vortex Control Self-Defense mimics that of warfare.

**Intelligence.** First, you must gather intelligence so you can make the right decision regarding your enemy. In warfare, this is done through methods such as espionage. In self-defense, it's better understood as "sizing up" your opponent.

Within a few seconds of studying your enemy, you can determine any weaknesses he has (such as obvious injuries), sense his fear (or lack thereof), assess his ability (speed, strength, skill), etc. You can also assess your surroundings and identify possible escape routes, available weapons, etc.

**Bombs.** After your initial assessment, assuming you feel that fighting is necessary, attack with bombs. The military uses planes and mortars. In Vortex Control Self-Defense, we use bomb-kicks.

**Infantry.** Finally, once the bombs have done their job, the infantry is sent in. This translates to the use of entry techniques and the fighting formula.

## Waterfall

The analogy of water going over the edge of a waterfall is often used to explain how to perform certain movements used in the techniques. The free-fall of water is also akin to grounding. Combing the three actions of waterfall, grounding, and vortex is extremely powerful.

## Weaponizing

The principle of weaponizing means to make as many of your movements as much like attacks as possible, even if they are primarily defensive or neutral. Here are some examples:

- Instead of just placing your foot down after a kick, stomp your opponent's knee or foot.
- When defending against an incoming strike, don't just block it. Instead, block it in a way that hurts your opponent as well. Punch his arm (a stop-hit), for example.
- Your intention may be to apply a lock, but you can make various strikes in the process.
- After hitting your opponent, hit him again while retracting your limb.

## Yin and Yang

The well-known Chinese Taoism concept of yin and yang is also applied in Vortex Control Self-Defense, where yin is "soft" and yang is "hard."

Soft does not equal weak, and it is the combination of soft and hard, fast and slow, light and heavy (grounded), etc. that will make your techniques work together.

Here are some examples to demonstrate the use of yin and yang in the context of Vortex Control Self-Defense. These are just a few examples of a concept that applies to everything in the universe.

- Tai Chi is very yin (slow and soft) in practice, and to the layman it may seem useless for combat, but if you speed the movements up to become yang (hard and fast), they can be devastating.
- In training, it's useful to use more yin and less yang. Doing things slowly (yin) first allows your mind and body to "soak in" the lessons. If you go straight to yang, not only will you learn poor technique, but your chances of injury while training will also be much higher.
- When an opponent strikes, you can receive his attack using yin, going with the flow of his motion. You may also defend against it using yang, attacking your opponent's limb as he strikes. A third option is to use a combination of yin and yang, where you receive the attack by flowing with it and then redirect the energy to counterattack.
- When you're using your hand to meet an attack, if your fingers face forward, it is considered yin. If your fingers face up, it's Yang. When your fingers are up, the hard, bony part of your hand is exposed, but when your fingers are forward it's not.

## BASIC STANCE

When stationary, stand with your feet a bit wider than shoulder width apart.

Hold the stick in your strongest hand and have your strong side as your lead. The bottom of your weapon should extend between one and two inches below your little finger.

Unless you're performing an action (attack or defense), hold your stick back over your shoulder. Your hand should be near your ear on the same side, and the tip of your weapon should point to your rear. Doing this will:

- keep your hand out of range of your opponent's strike (if he hits your hand you might drop your weapon; and
- give your strikes the greatest power and speed for attacking your primary target—namely your opponent's head.

Your rear hand is a backup for defense or secondary attack, and should be kept close to your centerline most of the time.

## STEPPING

Advancing with the stick is the same as in hand to hand combat.

Spring semi-forward stepping is used to close distance. In this technique, your back heel is up. This turns your calf muscle into a double spring—one behind your knee and one at your heel. Releasing these springs propels your whole body forward.

Take a small step forward with your lead foot and place your rear foot in the original position of your lead.

Your stance should never be exaggerated (too long or short).

Keep most of your weight on your rear leg. The heel of your front foot should land first, followed by the toes of both feet. This will keep you well-grounded and ready for the next move.

## THE KING OF STRIKES

In Kali Arnis, each strike angle is given a number. These number assignments are common to most lineages, including other weapon systems such as Escrima.

When it comes to stick-fighting, the best strike by far is the number seven. In Vortex Control Stick-Fighting, it has been dubbed the "king of strikes" and is the first strike you learn. It is also the one you will use most often.

Strikes one to six come in on angles to hit the meaty parts of your opponent. The number seven strike comes straight down between your eyes. With it, you own the centerline, and whoever owns the centerline has the advantage.

When used offensively, the strike targets your opponent's face or the top of his head. In a defensive capacity, it protects you from any angulated strike. To do the number seven strike, start in the basic stance. Bring your stick straight down the center into your target. As the stick comes down, bring your other hand up. This helps keep you balanced and is also a backup defense.

Practice this fundamental strike in a stationary position, with forward stepping, and as double hits.

Simple but very effective combinations can be made all along the number seven axis.

Here is one example:

- Double hit, straight thrust, and step though with an uppercut using the bottom of the stick.

### The Seven Defense

If your opponent uses an angled attack (either intentionally or in a poorly executed king strike) then your number seven (king) will win.

When you both use well-executed king strikes, then whoever is first to the target will have the advantage.

If you are not the first, then you must turn your attack into a defense.

**Note:** Theoretically, if both fighters use perfect number sevens at the same time, the tips of their sticks will clash. In reality, this is extremely unlikely.

To make the king strike defensive, place your rear hand behind your stick as you do the strike. If needed, you can turn slightly toward the angle your opponent's strike is coming on.

Do not turn more than 10°. It is the creation of triangles that makes the defense structure strong.

Another way to use the number seven in defense is if you are under pressure—if your opponent is holding your stick down, for example.

Just return to a number seven position. You may need to step back to create space and/or move your weapon in a circular motion to facilitate this.

The act of "returning to seven" is a simple and effective strategy to regain dominance, and is referred to more throughout this book.

**Related Chapters:**

- Basic Stance
- Stepping

## QUEEN STRIKE

A very important strike in Vortex Control Stick-Fighting is the queen strike.

The queen strike is derived from the abanico movement, as opposed the sword-type movement other strikes, such as the king strike.

Abanico is done by flicking your wrist so your stick follows a fan shape. This movement allows the stick to go around common defenses and strike at unexpected angles.

The queen strike is quicker but less powerful than the king. Its big advantage is that it can be used at close range. While the king is good when you have space, the queen is effective once your opponent moves in close and/or grabs your stick or wrist while your arm is down.

When your opponent grabs you, slap down on his hand and do the queen strike. The slap will pull your opponent into your strike as well as help to flick your strike into his face (left picture).

It is also very easy to defend against a strike from this position, which has the same structure as when you're using the king strike as a defense (right picture).

Although you want all strikes to be fast and well-aimed, this is more important with the queen strike. For example, aim for the eye when executing a head shot. You can practice in the air or with a small target by continuously making fast strikes to a single point.

The queen strike can be magnified by dropping into it (grounding). As you do the queen, quickly sink your weight and move back. This will straighten your opponent's arm, throw him off balance, give him a "whiplash" effect, and nullify his other arm.

**Queen Defense and Counters**

Defending against a queen strike is more difficult than with other strikes. The biggest problem is that you need to see the strike coming.

The seven defense can be used, but you need to angulate more than usual, since the queen strike can go around the centerline.

To counter this defense, attack with a king strike as follows.

You (the person on the left) strike with a queen strike while your opponent defends with a modified seven defense.

Use your left hand to cover his arms as you retract your stick and counter with a king strike (returning to seven).

If your stick is on his, you can defend against the queen strike by moving your stick away from your opponent's hand. This will nullify the pivot point his stick moves around. That is, your stick becomes a "wall" as opposed to being part of the pivot point.

To counter this defense, use your hand to hit your opponent's stick in the same direction he is moving it as he creates a gap. Hit it completely off your stick.

Once his stick is out of the way, you'll have many options, such as queen strikes or returning to seven.

**Note:** Pushing your opponent's stick away is not a preferred strategy, since it allows him to use the stick again. In most cases, it's better to take control of his stick.

**Related Chapters:**

- The King of Strikes

# STRIKE DRILLS

For the following drills, stand with your feet a little more than shoulder-width apart. Lead with your strong side and angle your body at 45° to your target. Point your feet toward your enemy.

The idea of this drill is to practice using circular forces. Roll your strikes using your waist. Most of your movement and power comes from your body motion, not your arm. Using only your arm and wrist limits your power. It's good for sport, to get fast points, but not very effective on the street. Big hits end fights.

These are primarily short-range strikes. Do not fully extend your arm when making them. You may get more distance, but will lose power at your shoulder. It will also make it easier for your opponent to manipulate your stick and/or grab arm.

## Cutting Strikes

The strikes in this drill are considered long-range ones, and are good entry blows.

Aim to hit your target with the upper couple of inches of your stick. The strikes should go through your opponent in a cutting motion. Taken together, first four strikes form an infinity symbol.

**Forehand to the head.** From the starting position, bring your stick down diagonally across your body. Your opponent's temple and eye are your primary targets.

**Backhand to the head.** Bring the stick up your left side to the top of your left shoulder, then continue down diagonally across your body to your bottom right.

**Forehand to the knee.** Bring your stick up to shoulder height and squat down to lower your body. Strike down at your opponent's knee.

**Backhand to the knee.** Raise the stick up to your left shoulder. Stay low.

Do a backhand strike to your opponent's knee.

**Repeat the previous four strikes a few times so you get used to using your waist.**

**Forehand Horizontal.** After strike four, come back up and bring your stick back to waist height. Drive the stick horizontally to your left side. Your intention is to hit your opponent's elbow, wrist, or floating ribs if he has kept them open.

**Backhand Horizontal.** Move the stick back to your right side, more or less along the same path, but in reverse.

**The King.** Finish off with the king strike.

## Bouncing Strikes

In this drill, you follow the same pattern as the cutting strikes drill, but the strikes are adapted for mid-range blows. At this range, you and your opponent are close enough to grab each other's weapons.

Bouncing strikes use a movement something between abanico and cutting strikes.

Contact is made from about halfway up the stick to the bottom of the top couple of inches.

Begin the first strike as before (forehand to the head). Instead of going through your opponent, your stick will make contact and then bounce off him.

Using the momentum of the ricochet, guide your stick over your head in a circular abanico style and then make the second strike.

The same ricochet action is done for all seven of the strikes. Here are strikes three and four.

Strikes five and six.

Strike seven.

## Rolling Strikes

This last set of strikes uses the same pattern again, but this time each strike is a double hit.

The double hit is achieved by rolling. Once the first strike crosses the center, you use your wrist to circle the strike over for a second hit before moving on to the next strike in the pattern. As an exercise, this move helps to develop flexibility, coordination, and strength in your wrist. In a fight, it is useful for making space, and/or as a way to exit if you think your opponent has had enough. Move back while doing it.

The number seven strike is not included in this drill.

The start of strike one is exactly the same as in the cutting strikes drill.

Once you cross center use your wrist to double up the strike and then continue to the other side.

Strike two is the same as strike one, but backhand. Strikes three and four are the same as strikes one and two, respectively, except that they are aimed at your opponent's knee.

In strikes five and six, the double-up action is a circular movement over your head.

## Strike Strategy

If you were to fight using only the strikes from these drills, the basic strategy would be to:

- Enter with cutting strikes.
- Batter your opponent with bouncing strikes.
- Exit with rolling strikes.

**Related Chapters:**

- The King of Strikes

## ABANICO DEFENSE

When both you and your opponent strike, but his timing is ahead of yours, you may choose to defend at the last instant. This defense works best when your opponent's strike is off center (not a pure seven). Both you and your opponent come in with overhead strikes. Your opponent's timing is just ahead of yours, so you quickly tap his weapon out of the way.

Use the abanico-style wrist flick coupled with the movement of your waist to renew your attack.

Whether you use a left or right tap depends on whether your opponent uses a number one or number two strike. You can close in as your opponent renews his attack.

## STICK PARRIES

When you are too close to use the abanico defense, stick parries are the answer. Deflect your opponent's attack (parry) and then counter with a strike or snatch.

If your opponent attacks with a number seven strike, you need to get off center to be able to parry it. To deflect on your right side, take a slightly angulated step forward and raise your hand a little so that your bent arm and stick form a triangle. This triangle will cause your opponent's attack to glide off. Do not angle your arm out. It will weaken the structure.

Once the attack has been deflected, counterattack (left picture below).

You can use your other hand to help guide your opponent's stick out of the way (right picture below). If you are ahead of his timing, your sticks may not even come into contact.

You may choose to go into a snatch. Here is one example.

When you need to deflect on your left side, point your stick over your left shoulder. The triangle will be maintained.

## Returning to Seven

In this variation of the stick parries drill, you and your opponent alternate attack and defense positions. You do not grab each other's sticks. Your opponent strikes at you with a number seven. Parry and counter with your own number seven. As you counter, your opponent must bring his stick back to a seven. You will be quicker, so he will be obliged to concede and defend. Your opponent deflects your number seven and counters with his own number seven.

Repeat the deflection and counter one for one.

**Important:** Always be mindful of returning to and controlling center. In stick-fighting, this means going back to a seven strike (returning to seven). Do what you have to do, but then come back to a seven. You may have to concede if your opponent is faster than you, but return to the seven.

You can come in from the side if needed, but always aim to dominate the center, and once you are in, don't go back out.

**Related Chapters:**

- Abanico Defense

## DEFENSE DRILL

The previous two styles of defense (parry and abanico) can be practiced as a flow drill with a partner. Here is a sample progression.

1. Attacker strikes with alternating number one and two strikes. Defender defends using parries. Repeat this a few times.
2. Attacker strikes with alternating number one and two strikes. Defender defends using the abanico defense. Repeat this a few times.
3. Attacker strikes with number one and two strikes at his discretion. Defender uses parries, and can also counter when ready.
4. Attacker strikes with number one and two strikes at his discretion. Defender uses the abanico defense and can also counter when ready.

### Related Chapters:

- Abanico Defense

# SNATCHES

Snatching is when you take your opponent's stick from him. When you are fighting stick-on-stick, using the king strike is going to beat an average opponent 90% of the time.

When your opponent knows what he is doing, using a snatch is your next best option. This is because most stick systems don't involve grabbing the stick, so doing so gives you a major advantage.

All snatches begin with the seven defense. Once you've blocked your opponent's attack, use your free hand to take control of his weapon.

**Note:** For most snatches to work, you need to get your opponent's hand to your stick. When your hand touches your opponent's stick you can prevent a snatch by creating a small space (see Queen Defense and Counters) or by jumping (see Double-Grab Drill).

In the following demonstrations, all the attacks are either number one or number two strikes. However, with slight adjustments, the snatches can be applied to different strike angles. Even if your opponent uses a perfect king strike, you can turn it into an angled strike by blocking it on one side or the other.

Unless otherwise stated, in all these demonstrations you are the person on the right.


**Snatch One: Stick on Stick**

Your opponent attacks with a number one strike. Block the strike.

Grab the top of your opponent's stick with your left hand. Use an overhand grip (palm facing down).

Pull your opponent's stick down towards the outside of his guard, so that it's horizontal. The two sticks should form a cross, with your stick being close to your opponent's hand.

Push your opponent's stick into his face using a vortex motion, and then pry it out of his hand. Do so by using a waterfall action to push it past the outside of his shoulder. Finish with a butt strike (a strike with the bottom of your stick) to your opponent's face.

**Snatch Two: Fist on Fist**

Your opponent attacks with a number one strike. Block the strike.

Grab the top of your opponent's stick with your left hand. Use an overhand grip.

As you pull your opponent's stick down into the cross, place your right fist on the back of his right fist.

Push your opponent's stick into his face and then pry it out of his hand by pushing it past the outside of his shoulder.

Finish with a strike to your opponent's face.

**Snatch Three: Stick Lever**

Your opponent attacks with a number one strike. Block the strike.

Grab the top of your opponent's stick with your left hand. Use an overhand grip.

Strike your opponent in the face with the butt of your stick, using a slight hooking motion.

Continue along that path so that your right wrist lands on your opponent's right wrist. The end of your stick should be underneath your left armpit. Using your stick as a fulcrum, pry your opponent's stick out of his hand by pulling it down towards your left with your left hand.

You can thrust the butt of your stick into your opponent's face a few times if you need to.

### Snatch Four: Wrist Grab

Your opponent attacks with a number one strike. Block the strike.

Grab your opponent's right wrist with your left hand and twist his arm slightly, so that his elbow faces the ground. Using your left arm as a guide, draw your stick back.

Follow your stick back down along your arm to hit your opponent's stick out of his hand. You can also use your forearm to make the disarming hit.

### Snatch Five: Twist and Hit

Your opponent attacks with a number two strike. Block the strike.

Grab your opponent's stick between his hand and your stick. Use an underhand grip (palm facing up).

Twist your opponent's stick down and continue to twist clockwise. This on its own may disarm him.

If not, use your lower left forearm (or the bottom of your stick) to strike his right wrist.

You can also use the back of your right elbow to strike the back of your opponent's right elbow.

### Snatch Six: But Strike

Your opponent attacks with a number two strike. Block the strike.

Grab your opponent's right wrist using an underhand grip.

Use your forearm to strike downward and knock your opponent's stick out of his hand.

**Snatch Seven: Twist and Pressure**

Your opponent attacks with a number two strike. Block the strike.

Twist the bottom of your stick clockwise and over your opponent's stick. At the same time bring your left hand up underneath your opponent's right forearm.

Apply downward pressure with your stick and upward pressure with your left hand to disarm your opponent.

If this opposing pressure is not enough, draw your opponent's stick straight out towards you by pulling your stick back.

Hold your opponent's stick between your right arm and your body, and then use your left hand and a twist of your waist to push on the back of his right hand and move it to your right.

If that is still not enough, bring the bottom of your opponent's stick up and over his right hand. Twist back to your left and strike your opponent as you do so.

### Snatch Eight: Hit and Twist

Your opponent attacks with a number two strike. Block the strike.

Grab your opponent's stick and push the top of it into his face.

Twist your opponent's stick counterclockwise to your left, using your stick as a fulcrum.

As you do this, let the stick "spin" in your right hand, so that you finish with an overhand grip.

Once your opponent's stick is toward your left side, tighten your grip. Keep twisting until the stick comes out of your opponent's grip, and aim the bottom of it towards his groin. Not only will this hit him, it will also make it easier to get the stick out of his grip.

### Snatch Nine: Arm Lever

Your opponent attacks with a number two strike. Block the strike.

Grab your opponent's stick and then lower it, so you can thrust the tip of your stick into him.

Do a second thrust past your opponent's head (or if you missed the first one) and then use your arm as the fulcrum point to disarm your opponent, in the same way as in snatch eight.

Alternatively, you can punch your opponent.

### Snatch Ten: Push and Pull

Your opponent attacks with a number two strike. Block the strike.

Grab your opponent's stick and push the top of it into his face.

Change your grip so that your palm faces your left, and then pull your opponent's stick back towards you so that his hand is up against your stick.

Push towards your opponent to make his arm collapse, and then pull back to take the stick.

### Snatch Eleven: Reverse Wrist Grab

Your opponent attacks with a number two strike. Block the strike.

Grab your opponent's stick between your stick and his hand. Use an underhand grip.

Rotate your opponent's stick to your left so that your two sticks make a cross.

Release your grip on your opponent's stick and grab his wrist. Your hand should pass between the two sticks.

Use your forearm to knock the stick out of your opponent's hand.

**Snatch Twelve: Weave and Pull**

Your opponent attacks with a number two strike. Block the strike.

Weave your hand over your opponent's stick between your stick and his hand and then under your opponent's wrist to your left.

Maneuver your stick so it is positioned horizontally over your opponent's forearm and then grab the end of it with your left hand.

Pull towards yourself to dislodge your opponent's stick.

The same weaving maneuver can be used on your opponent's upper arm. Apply a painful lock with downward pressure. You can then slide your stick back to your opponent's wrist to disarm him as before.

**Snatch Thirteen: Wrist Slam**

Your opponent attacks with a number two strike. Block the strike.

Grab your opponent's stick and lower it so you can thrust the tip of your stick into him.

Pass your stick under your opponent's arm and toward your left side. As you do this, quickly put your right hand on top of his hand.

Maneuver the bottom of your stick so it is on top of your opponent's lower arm.

Use your left hand to slam down on your stick where it is on your opponent's arm.

An alternative to slamming down on your stick is to push the top of your stick into your opponent's head.

**Related Chapters:**

- The King of Strikes
- Queen Strike
- Double-Grab Scenarios

# GRAB AND STRIKE DRILLS

In the snatches chapter, you learned how stick grabbing enables you to take your opponent's weapon. In the exercises in this chapter, you'll be grabbing your opponent's stick and then moving it out of the way so you can strike him.

This chapter also delves into advanced strikes. In this demonstration, you are in the position of the person on the right in the pictures.

This is all one drill, but has been split into three parts—basic, intermediate, advanced—for ease of learning.

### Basic Grab and Strike Drill

This drill makes use of the seven cutting strikes as well as a modified queen strike.

Your opponent strikes with a number seven hit. Defend with a number seven so that the top of your opponent's stick will be inside your guard.

Grab his stick with your left hand using an overhand grip above the point where the two sticks meet.

Prepare to strike by pulling his stick to the left side of your head while bringing your stick to the outside of your left side.

Strike with a number four hit to his knee.

Place your stick back on your opponent's to form a cross. Change your left-hand grip to an underhand grip below the point where the two sticks meet.

Hit his lead knee using a number three strike.

Place your stick back on his to form a cross.

Prepare for your next strike by pulling his stick down to your left side and over your left shoulder, then strike with a number two hit.

Pull your stick back over your left shoulder. Place your stick back on your opponent's to form a cross.

Change your left hand to an overhand grip below the point where the two sticks meet and then pull your opponent's stick down and to your right.

Strike with a number one hit.

Place your stick back on your opponent's to form a cross, and then move your left hand above the point where the two sticks meet. Use an overhand grip.

Lower his stick a bit and then use a queen strike to hit his face. Your strike should go over his stick.

Change your left-hand grip to an underhand grip below the point where the two sticks meet and then pull your opponent's stick to your left as you pull yours to your right.

Strike your opponent with a number one strike and then pull your stick back and to your right.

Bring the sticks back into a cross and then change to an overhand grip.

Push your opponent's stick down and to your right, then strike with a number seven hit.

Bring the sticks back into a cross.

## Intermediate Grab and Strike Drill

Rolling and abanico strikes are used in this stage of the drill.

Start in the finishing position from the basic grab and strike drill, sticks in a cross.

Push your opponent's stick down and strike with a rolling number seven strike.

The rolling strike should travel down the outside of your opponent's right side.

It should then continue on a circular path, coming up on the outside of your left shoulder and down, so that your stick crosses on your opponent's stick horizontally.

Step to the outside of your opponent's guard. Use your left hand to cover your opponent's right forearm and then strike him in the face, either with your fist or with the bottom of your stick.

Use your left hand to take an underhand grip on your opponent's stick. Pull his stick up and strike him in the face with your right hand (or stick). At the same time, change to an overhand grip with your left hand.

Push your opponent's stick back down and do an abanico hit to the right side of his head.

Rotate your stick in the opposite direction to ma an abanico hit to the left side of your opponent's head. Whilst rotating your stick, hit your opponent in the face with his own stick.

Return your stick to a number seven position and continue through with a rolling hit.

This hit should finish with you holding your stick at waist height, pointing it towards your opponent.

### Advanced Grab and Strike Drill

This final stage of the grab and strike drill uses slashing and stabbing strikes. Start by hitting your opponent with the top of his own stick as you bring your stick back up to your right shoulder.

Do a number three strike which slashes through him and ends at your left hip.

Hit your opponent with the top of his own stick and then do a number four strike through him.

Finish the strike at your right hip and then pull your opponent's stick down.

Do an upwards slashing strike through his head, from bottom right to top left. The tip of your stick should end up behind your left shoulder.

Hit your opponent with the top of his own stick and then pull it down to your left.

Do a horizontal back-hand strike through your opponent's head and quickly follow up by hitting him with the top of his own stick in a semi-circular motion from (your opponent's) right to left.

As you complete this strike, bring the tip of your stick near your left hip.

Use a queen strike to hit your opponent's face. Your strike should go over his stick.

Use another queen strike to hit your opponent's stick away.

As you do so, quickly cover his right hand with your left and then use a hooking motion from (your) right to left to drive the tip of your stick through your opponent's face.

Continue to thrust your stick past your opponent's face.

Once the tip of your stick is past your opponent's face, bring your right hand to your own upper left side while turning the tip of your stick back towards your opponent. As you do so, move your left hand also comes up between your chin and right hand.

Thrust the tip of your stick towards your opponent's face as you pull your left hand back to defend your head.

Use an abanico movement to bring your stick back toward you and down in a circular movement in order to hit your opponent in the groin.

Let your stick bounce back and over.

Use the momentum to hit your opponent in the top of the head.

Start to step back with your right foot as you bring your stick up and out.

Strike your opponent with the tip of your stick using a right overhand thrust.

This completes the full grab and strike drill.

## GRAB AND STRIKE DEFENSE DRILLS

### Grab and Strike Defense Drill One

This flow drill shows how to defend against someone who grabs your stick and strikes. It demonstrates defense against the first four strikes from the previous chapter (grab and strike) which you can then adapt to any strike. It also contains a few examples (of the many that are possible) of snatch opportunities along the way.

In this demonstration, you take the position of the person on the right in the pictures. The person on the left is doing the grab and strike drill from the previous chapter and you are defending against his strikes. Strike at your opponent with a number seven hit. Your opponent defends with a number seven so that the top of your stick will end up inside his guard.

Your opponent grabs your stick with his left hand using an overhand grip above the point where the two sticks meet. He pulls back to strike you with a number four hit.

As your opponent strikes, use your left hand to block his right hand.

At the same time, pull the bottom of your stick down so that his stick hits it between your right and his left hand. Return to the cross position.

Your opponent switches his left-hand grip to an underhand grip below the point where the two sticks meet.

Your opponent pulls back to strike with a number three hit.

As the strike comes in, use your left hand to hit down on your opponent's left wrist from the outside of his guard. This will move your stick down to block the strike.

It is important to push his stick down the right amount. If you don't push the stick down far enough, it will not block the strike, and it may hit your hand. If you push it down too much, it will knock the top of your stick back into you. Ideally, you want the stick to hit your opponent's hand.

From this position you can do a queen strike. This is not part of the drill.

**Training Tip:** Practice these first movements until you're proficient before moving on.

You both return to the cross position, and then your opponent pulls your stick down and to your right as he pulls back for a number two strike.

As the strike comes in, simultaneously raise the bottom of your stick and use your left hand to hit down on your opponent's stick. This will ensure your opponent's stick doesn't hit your hand.

Return to the cross position. Your opponent changes to a forward grip. Your opponent pulls your stick down and to his right as he pulls back for a number one hit.

As the strike comes in, turn your body to the left and bend at your knees as you raise the bottom of your stick to protect your head.

If you need to, use your right hand to pull your opponent's stick down. This will ensure your opponent's stick doesn't hit your hand.

Throughout the whole Grab and Strike Defense Drill, there are opportunities to strike, snatch, etc. The following examples outline small fraction of the possibilities to give you an idea of what can be done. Once you're proficient at the drill, progress to adding additional attacks.

**Variation One**

As your opponent grabs your stick for his first strike, grab his stick towards the tip, using an overhand grip.

Use your stick as a fulcrum and pry your opponent's stick out of his hand by circling it counterclockwise. As you do the circling movement, allow your opponent's stick to spin in your palm and/or fingers, so that you're able to smoothly change grip as needed.

**Variation Two**

As your opponent grabs your stick for his first strike, grab his stick at a point between his hand and your stick using an underhand grip.

Circle the stick clockwise until your opponent's palm faces up. Use your right hand to strike downward on your opponent's wrist and disarm him.

**Variation Three**

If you were unable to rotate the stick clockwise, as in example two (perhaps your opponent's grip was too strong), reverse your grip. That is, use an underhand grip, but with your elbow pointing up.

Rotate your opponent's stick counterclockwise and place your right fist on the back of his right fist.

Push your opponent's hand towards his face. This will tangle him up. Continue to push.

## Variation Four

Block your opponent's third strike in the drill. Rotate the bottom of your stick over your opponent's so it hits down on his right hand. At the same time, use your left hand to pull up on your opponent's right hand.

## Variation Five

After you have blocked your opponent's third strike in the drill, grab your stick near the tip. Use an underhand grip, so that your elbow faces up. Rotate your stick counterclockwise until it's vertical, and then push it into your opponent's face.

**Variation Six**

Block your opponent's fourth strike in the drill and then, from the defensive position, use your stick as a fulcrum and pry your opponent's stick out of his hand.

You can also push your opponent's stick into his head.

**Grab and Strike Defense Drill Two**

This drill is the same as the grab and strike defense drill, except the defender is more proactive. He hits the attacker's hand off his (the defender's) stick and then counterattacks.

In the following examples, you are the person on the left.

As your opponent does the first strike in the drill (a number four), use your left hand to block his right hand. At the same time, pull the bottom of your stick down, so that your opponent's stick hits it between your right and his left hand.

Use your left hand to slap his left hand off your stick.

Continue with the grab and strike defense as normal.

As your opponent does the second strike (a number three), use your left hand to block his right hand. At the same time, pull the bottom of your stick down, so that your opponent's stick hits it between your right and his left hand. Use your left hand to slap his left hand off your stick.

As his third strike comes in, deflect it as usual, then bring your stick back over into a king strike.

Deflect the final strike as usual.

Then bring your stick back over into a king strike.

### Grab and Strike Defense Drill Three

In this drill, you practice getting your opponent's stick and using it against him, and as in the previous drill, you also practice going back to seven (the king strike).

It's better to hit your opponent with his stick than your hand. It will hurt him more and give you control of his stick.

To increase his pain, aim for bony areas, rather than muscle, when striking your opponent with his stick as opposed to muscle.

From the first defensive position, use your right hand to grab your opponent's stick in the space between your stick and his right hand.

Use his stick to hit his arm from below. Adopt the seven position and then continue to the second defensive position.

Grab the upper section of your opponent's stick and bring it up and over to hit his left arm. At the same time, place your stick on top of his to come into the seven position.

This will also give you more leverage when you're hitting him with his own stick.

As you adopt the third defensive position, swing your stick into the number seven position and use his stick to hit his left arm from above.

For extra strength, place your stick on top of his as you do this.

You can then thrust or do other strikes.

From the last defensive position, use your left hand to grab the upper section of your opponent's stick.

As you return your stick to the number seven position, use your opponent's stick to strike down on his left arm.

For extra strength, place your stick on top of his as you do this. You can then thrust or do other strikes.

**Related Chapters:**

- Queen Strike
- Grab and Strike Drills
- The King of Strikes

# BREAK-OUTS

This chapter demonstrates a few simple techniques you can use to escape when your opponent grabs your stick.

## Butt-Thrust Breakout

This is a good option for when your stick is more horizontal than vertical. It makes use of butt strikes (strikes made with the bottom of your stick), which are extremely effective in close combat. Use your right hand to pull your opponent's wrist towards you as you thrust the butt of your stick into his torso. You can also do this without the thrust to the torso. From this position, you can go into a simple arm-break and/or butt-strike combination. For the arm-break, pull his wrist back toward you with your left hand as you apply forward pressure on his elbow with your right arm.

For the butt-strike combination, bring the bottom of your stick over your opponent's arm, hitting the side of his face with the bottom (the butt) of your stick. Slam your forearm down into the crook of his elbow to jerk him down, and then come back up into his jaw with the butt of your stick.

**Elbow Breakout One**

Use this technique when your stick is more vertical and your opponent has grabbed it, leaving little or no gap between his and your hands.

Bring the bottom of your stick up and in toward him, so your forearms are aligned and touching. Then slam the bottom of your stick/forearm down on his lower arm as you do queen strike to his head.

This should be one smooth movement. Move the bottom of your stick toward him in a vortex motion.

By using a vortex, you move around his wrist, following the natural movement of his body.

There is no need to fight him with force.

**Elbow Breakout Two**

A similar movement to Elbow Breakout One can be used no matter how big the gap between your and your opponent's hands is. Grab onto either your stick or his wrist and then move the bottom of your stick over your opponent's arm in a vortex motion.

Bring it down toward him and onto his arm. From here, you can do a queen strike or the butt-strikes combination, among many other options.

**Related Chapters:**

- Queen Strike

## DOUBLE-GRAB SCENARIOS

When both you and your opponent grab each other's sticks, the person who knows what to do next and does it first will be the victorious one.

### Gaining Advantage with Distance

When you're both at striking distance (or further), you're equal in terms of advantageous distance. When your opponent moves in and gets hold of your stick, it's bad for you.

If you move in and grab his stick as well, then you'll be back to being equal.

The best position is to have your hand inside his guard. Amongst other things, it allows you to do the queen strike.

**Double-Grab Adaptations**

The same techniques that have been presented so far in this book can be adapted to double-grab situations. This chapter showcases a small number of these adaptations.

In these examples, you are the person on the left.

**Hit-and-Twist Snatch**

You both grab each other's' sticks in the high position.

Push towards your opponent with the intent of hitting him with the top of his stick. As you do this, change the grip of your left hand and do a hit-and-twist snatch.

**Twist-and-Hit Snatch**

Your opponent grabs your stick high and you grab his low, with an underhand grip.

Pull the top of your opponent's stick down with a vortex motion. This will often be enough to snatch the stick from him.

If not, smash the bottom of your stick down on his lower arm as you pull his stick up with your left hand.

**Fist Snatch**

You grab your opponent's stick high and he grabs yours low.

Pull the top of his stick down and do a fist snatch.

**Elbow Breakout**

You grab your opponent's stick high and he grabs yours low.

Bring your stick up and then slam your elbow down on his arm in a vortex motion.

**Returning to Seven**

If you're the one in a disadvantageous position and get closed in on, you need to create distance so you can return to seven.

In the following demonstrations, you are the person on the right.

Step back to create space. As you do, bring the butt of your stick down. It is your arm that should straighten. Do not pull your stick back—you don't want to give up ground.

Once the butt of your stick is down, step forward again as you return to seven.

**Double-Grab Countering Scenarios**

The closing-in counter is a good move for when your opponent closes in on you.

As he does so, counter by putting your left elbow on his right fist and then twisting to your right.

This demonstrates how you can counter the closing-in counter.

Hold each other's sticks in the high position. As you close in on your opponent, he does the elbow counter as previously described. Counter this by allowing the motion to happen and keeping hold of your stick, then pull up on your opponent's stick while smashing your stick into his hand.

Push the top of your opponent's stick into his face so you can change grip and finish with a snatch.

### Double-Grab Drill

This drill is a good way to hone your reactions when you have hold of each other's sticks.

In this explanation, you are the person on the left.

Start with both of you holding each other's sticks and then begin to apply a fist-on-fist snatch to your opponent.

From the position shown in the first picture below, you need to push towards your opponent so you can change grip with your left hand and then apply the snatch.

As your opponent feels the snatch being applied, he steps back and then returns to seven which you block with your stick.

Change the grip of your left hand. Don't forget to push your opponent's stick towards him first. Since you changed your grip, your opponent senses what you want to do (that is, hit his arm with his own stick). To prevent this, he quickly moves his left hand to the outer side of your stick.

You change your grip again so you can apply a twist-and-hit snatch.

Your opponent feels it so he steps back and returns to seven, which
you block again.

This puts your left hand in a bad position, so push towards your
opponent and change your grip. Go to hit your opponent's left hand.
To avoid getting hit, your opponent jumps to the other side of your
stick.

Change grip with your left hand and go for the fist-on-fist snatch to
repeat the drill.

Once you and your opponent have gotten the hang of it, swap roles.

# THANKS FOR READING

**Dear reader,**

Thank you for reading *Practical Arnis Stick Fighting*.

If you enjoyed this book, please leave a review where you bought it. It helps more than most people think.

**Don't forget your FREE book chapters!**

You will also be among the first to know of FREE review copies, discount offers, bonus content, and more.

Go to:

https://offers.SFNonfictionBooks.com/Free-Chapters

Thanks again for your support.

# REFERENCES

Abenir, F. (2014). *Eskrima Street Defense: Practical Techniques for Dangerous Situations*. Tambuli Media.

Anderson, D. (2013). *De-Fanging The Snake: A Guide To Modern Arnis Disarms*. CreateSpace Independent Publishing Platform.

Anderson, D. (2013). *Filipino Martial Arts - The Core Basics, Structure, & Essentials*. CreateSpace Independent Publishing Platform.

Anderson, D. (2014). *Trankada: The Joint Locking Techniques & Tapi-Tapi of Modern Arnis*. CreateSpace Independent Publishing Platform.

Buot, S. (2015). *Balintawak Eskrima*. Allegro Editions.

Diega, A. Ricketts, C. (2002). *The Secrets of Kalis Ilustrisimo: The Filipino Fighting Art Explained*. Tuttle Publishing.

Godhania, K. (2012). *Eskrima: Filipino Martial Art*. Crowood.

Gould, D. (2016). *Lameco Eskrima: The Legacy of Edgar G. Sulite*. Tambuli Media.

Medina, D. (2014). *The Secret Art of Derobio Escrima: Martial Art of the Philippines*. Tambuli Media.

Paman, J. (2007). *Arnis Self-Defense: Stick, Blade, and Empty-Hand Combat Techniques of the Philippines*. Blue Snake Books.

Pentecost, D. (2016). *Put 'Em Down. Take 'Em Out!: Knife Fighting Techniques From Folsom Prison*. Allegro Editions.

Presas, R. (1983). *Modern Arnis: The Filipino Art of Stick Fighting*. Black Belt Communications.

Preto, L. (2016). *Multiple opponent combat: 10 lesson program with one handed weapons*. CreateSpace Independent Publishing Platform.

Wiley, M. (2011). *Secrets of Cabales Serrada Escrima*. Tuttle Publishing.

Wiley, M. (2015). *Mastering Eskrima Disarms*. Tambuli Media.

# AUTHOR RECOMMENDATIONS

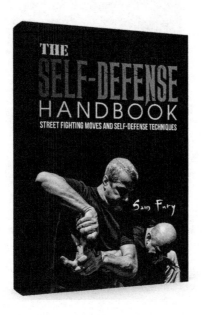

**Discover all the Street Fighting Techniques You Need**

Start learning what you need to win, because there ain't no rules on the streets.

**Get it now.**

www.SFNonfictionBooks.com/Self-Defense-Handbook

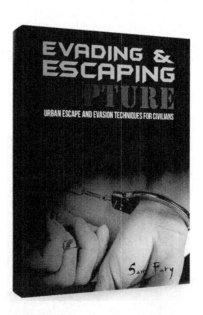

**Teach Yourself Escape and Evasion Tactics**

Discover the skills you need to evade and escape capture, because you never know when they will save your life.

**Get it now.**

www.SFNonfictionBooks.com/Evading-Escaping-Capture

# ABOUT SAM FURY

Sam Fury has had a passion for survival, evasion, resistance, and escape (SERE) training since he was a young boy growing up in Australia.

This led him to years of training and career experience in related subjects, including martial arts, military training, survival skills, outdoor sports, and sustainable living.

These days, Sam spends his time refining existing skills, gaining new skills, and sharing what he learns via the Survival Fitness Plan website.

www.SurvivalFitnessPlan.com

amazon.com/author/samfury

goodreads.com/SamFury

facebook.com/AuthorSamFury

instagram.com/AuthorSamFury

youtube.com/SurvivalFitnessPlan

Printed in Great Britain
by Amazon

33324429R00059